BIG SKY JOURNAL

# THE NEW MONTANA CABIN

# BIG SKY JOURNAL

# THE NEW MONTANA CABIN

## Contemporary Approaches to the Traditional Western Retreat

## SEABRING DAVIS

## TWODOT®

GUILFORD, CONNECTICUT
HELENA, MONTANA
AN IMPRINT OF THE GLOBE PEQUOT PRESS

**A · TWODOT® · BOOK**

Copyright © 2008 by Seabring Davis

TwoDot is a registered trademark of Morris Book Publishing, LLC.

Illustration credits: pp. i, 64 courtesy Kipp Halvorsen, Faure Halvorsen Architects; pp. ii-
iii © Shutterstock; p. viii courtesy Gordon Gregory; pp. 28, 53 courtesy Kyle Tage, Locati
Architects; pp. 29-37, 52-63, 100-111 © Roger Wade, styling by Debra Grahl; p. 38 courtesy
Thor Arnold, zimtor architecture; p. 101 courtesy Joseph Magaddino Architecture; p. 113
courtesy Brian H. Brothers, AIA. All others as noted in the text.

Text design by Sheryl P. Kober

Library of Congress Cataloging-in-Publication Data

Davis, Seabring.
  Big sky journal : the new Montana cabin : contemporary approaches to the traditional
Western retreat / Seabring Davis.
     p. cm.
  ISBN 978-0-7627-4696-5
  1. Vacation homes—Montana. I. Big sky journal. II. Title. III. Title: New Montana cabin.
  NA7575.D38 2008
  728.7'309786—dc22

                                                                              2008008474

Printed in China

10 9 8 7 6 5 4 3 2 1

# CONTENTS

# ACKNOWLEDGMENTS

The making of any book relies on a group of people who are often unseen and, therefore, unsung. For this project I'm grateful to those behind-the-scenes folks who have made available to the public this collection of homes that represent Montana. This book is both a celebration of these beautiful structures and a cultural documentation of our society's love of nesting. We are fortunate to live in a time when such luxuries are possible.

First, thank you to Jared Swanson, the publisher of *Big Sky Journal*, whose tireless optimism and business acumen has bolstered the magazine to a new level of success. His faith in me as an editor and writer continually inspires me to work harder.

Second, the photographers who contributed to this book have been invaluable. Of course, this project would not have been possible without their gorgeous images and I'm grateful to all of them. Lynn Donaldson, Tom Ferris, Gordon Gregory, J K Lawrence, and Roger Wade and Debbie Grahl—thank you for all your work!

I'm also grateful to my friend and fellow editor, Carter G. Walker, for her attentive ears, keen eyes, and ultimate patience; to my husband Colin for his unflagging support; and to Allen Jones, esteemed writer and patient editor, who believed that this book was a good idea.

Finally, I appreciate the opportunity to write about the incredible talent pool of architects, builders, interior designers, and artisans in Montana and the region. Special thanks to Diana Beattie, Candace Tillotson-Miller, Locati Architects, and Merle Adams.

# INTRODUCTION

"I went to the woods because I wished to live deliberately, to front only the essential facts of life, and see if I could learn what it had to teach, and not, when I came to die, discover that I had not lived."

—Henry David Thoreau, from *Walden; or, Life in the Woods*

The idea of a "cabin in the woods," whether romanticized by Henry David Thoreau or Laura Ingalls Wilder, conjures up the essence of living simply. It is a way to be close to nature, yet safe from harm. In a cabin the relationship between man and the natural world is tenuous, making life seem all the more precious and the wildness that we may fear or embrace that much closer to the door.

Of course, the earliest cabins were built for shelter from these harsh elements rather than any romantic notions of reconnecting with nature. For centuries people around the world made cabins using the most abundant and available materials, such as logs, stone, and wood. Throughout Europe's timber-rich land, log cottages were common, while remnants of makeshift stone-and-mud cabins dating back to the 1500s can still be found in Scotland. Historic writings note that cabin construction was typical to rural areas where their inhabitants were nomadic or simply not able to own property.

Along the American frontier cabins were also typically built as temporary housing, meant for use only until pioneers could afford to build something more substantial. The early English settlers relied on stonemasonry, but when Swedish immigrants arrived in North America about two decades after the Mayflower, they introduced a hand-hewn, stacked, notched construction that prevails even today. Other cultures influenced building practices, adjusting designs to accommodate regional needs.

Somewhere along the way, the cabin became symbolic to Americans. They were not popular until the late 1700s, when westward expansion began in earnest, yet by the mid-1800s the association of the cabin as emblematic of the American spirit was well established. President Lincoln touted his upbringing in a log cabin as a political tool to prove that he was the voice of the common man; Thoreau used his cabin on Walden Pond to promote his writings about returning to America's lost wilderness; and Wilder's

"Little House" stories portrayed the undaunted pioneer spirit that claimed this country. These layers of association built an image of the cabin—whether we are aware of it or not—as a structure that represents honesty, nature, and courage.

By definition, a cabin is a small house made of wood, usually a one-story dwelling of crude or simple construction. But somewhere along the way, the notion of the cabin as a utilitarian structure shifted. With the advent of industrialization in the late 1700s, Americans embraced technology, yet soon yearned for a time when life moved at a slower pace. By the 1930s the wealthy retreated from the pressures and daily strain of modern life to pastoral safe havens. In the East the great North Woods of New York's Adirondacks were one of the most notable refuges for city dwellers, while the West offered Yellowstone National Park, with its "Wonderland" appeal, and later the "dude" ranches that exposed thousands of would-be cowboys to the slow, easy pace of moving with the rhythms of the day. Outdoor recreation—particularly hunting, fishing, and hiking—became central to all these pursuits. With this idea of cabin as retreat, an American icon was formed, symbolizing freedom and humble living.

Today, of course, there is a vast difference between the roughed early cabins and contemporary structures. No longer a makeshift dwelling, the new cabin is a well-designed home that is often filled with the luxuries of our modern lifestyle. Our concept of simplicity has changed, too: No longer do we merely seek shelter, but also comfort and convenience, even luxury.

Still, what remains is the concept of paring down our complex lives and trading the frenzy of daily business for a quiet place where we are simply safe from harm. We seek to reconnect with the land, whether through materials used for construction, in the building site, or in the ease of moving between indoor and outdoor living. From a 120-square-foot structure tucked into a forest to a 7,000-square-foot log mansion on a mountaintop, the nostalgic component of the cabin prevails.

If there can be a defining element in the new Montana cabin, "place" is it: the notion that we are all free to enjoy the openness—the sky, mountains, rivers, and forests—while respecting the land and its history. To experience place gives us identity, which we draw not just from knowing the names of characters who "settled the West" or the dates of significant events, but also from re-creating elements of the built history that remains: the sod-roof houses, handmade log cabins, steep-gabled cottages, cobbled-together utility buildings, and hand-hewn barns that still dot the Montana landscape. These structures are leftovers of a lost way of life, when there seemed to be a tangible Manifest Destiny.

Though today's cabins are a far cry from those pragmatic structures of another era, in them there is the same reverence for simplicity. Whether the materials are reclaimed timbers from an 1870s barn, new board and batten, or recycled cedar shakes, piece-by-piece and board-by-board we reconnect with history, with each other, and with the natural world.

The homes in this book reflect a reverence for the land. They are not all log cabins—some have been reclaimed, restacked, and restored; some are sustainably built; and some apply traditional vernacular designs in new ways—but they all cherish the notion of simpler times while looking to the future.

## CHAPTER 1

# RETRO COZY

Photography by Gordon Gregory

It was the passing of her father that brought Carol Smith to Montana. In his will he'd left her his fishing cabin on the upper Yellowstone River, where he'd retreated all his life. Carol and her husband, Mike, flew in from Chicago to see the cabin and decide what should be done with it.

The couple landed in Jackson, Wyoming, and took the scenic route through Yellowstone National Park and the northern entrance at Gardiner. The drive was lovely, but it was when they entered Paradise Valley from the southern end that Carol burst into tears.

"I'd never seen anything so beautiful," she said, "and I knew at that moment what my father had loved about this place."

Though the Smiths sold the fishing cabin, the allure of Montana was what Carol's father passed on to her. She and Mike returned for vacations with their young children beginning in the early 1990s. At first they rented homes and then built one of their own, which they later sold. Along the way Carol and

Mike made the decision to retire in Montana when their kids were grown. That decision led them to a magical property in Bridger Canyon, where they began plans to build a dream home.

While waiting for the main house to be completed, Carol adopted the "Cozy Cabin," as she lovingly refers to it. The 1960s log house is nestled in the hillside, with a flight of stairs that leads to the wide front porch that overlooks the Bridger Range. Constructed of lodgepole pine harvested from the property, the exterior is painted a classic Forest Service dark brown. The gently sloped roof creates a low-profile structure that respects its serene surroundings.

There is a historic farmhouse on the property, but Carol noticed that it is drafty and cold during the winter months. Instead, she chose the funky cabin for its natural warmth and comfort, and has thoughtfully crafted it as a gathering place for her family and friends.

"In my life, the most important thing is for our family to be together," Carol said. "Coming to Montana over the years has done that. This is how families stay strong and close."

Carol worked with Swanson Construction of Bozeman to renovate the cabin and freshen it up, but made minimal changes to the floor plan. The exposed logs, hardwood floors, and low pine-plank ceiling enhance the warmth of the home. A double-sided stone fireplace divides the living room from the dining and kitchen area.

Not counting the front porch, the cabin is about 1,200 square feet. The Smith's three children—all now nearly grown—share a bedroom and a bathroom. The master bedroom down the hall is smaller, but it has a window with a view of the quiet valley to the west. A filmy white curtain filters the afternoon sunlight.

To combat the low ceilings and smaller spaces, Carol lightened and brightened each room with whitewashed walls and simple furnishings. Original acrylic paintings by Livingston artist Edd Enders hang in different rooms, adding a jolt of color to the soft palette of paint. Known for his impressionistic landscapes and "rural urbanscapes" that depict the

**In contrast to some of today's high-profile homes, this mid-twentieth-century cabin stays true to the simple roots of the region. Nestled in the hillside—near a dilapidated barn, chicken coop, and loading chute—it was likely a bunkhouse for the hired hands on a larger cattle ranch in Bridger Canyon. The cabin is built of lodgepole pine logs that were harvested from the property and then hand-peeled, stained dark brown, and stacked with chinking. The gabled roof is slightly angled to shed heavy snow. It was frugally built in order to conserve materials and its low height helps keep the house more efficiently heated.**

industrial edges of small towns, his work is a reflection of an insider's Montana, full of Big Sky scenery and quirkiness.

Carol pores through building and design magazines and takes pleasure in scavenging at dusty antiques shops. The trophies of her hunting are displayed throughout the cabin—a blend of cottage and country antiques with modern functionality. She calls them tchotchkes, waving them off with a laugh, but each ceramic figurine—a grizzly bear, an owl, a Hereford cow, a bison, or a wild turkey—is one more souvenir of her love for the wildness of this state. She talks of the moose that skirts around the perimeter of the cabin, the sandhill crane couple that walks down the gravel road on summer evenings, the

Opposite: An accent of teal paint on the gable complements the logs' classic Forest Service dark brown and adds a retro flair that celebrates the cabin's mid-twentieth-century kitsch.

Constructed in the 1960s, the lower level of the cabin is made from board and batten,
accented by a vintage wagon wheel and cheerful flower boxes.

bald eagles that soar overhead, and the trout in the ponds on the property.

Behind the cabin, Carol points out the dilapidated barn, a falling-down shed, and the old outhouse (a two-seater) that is overgrown with hop vines. She will leave them all as they stand, and maybe someday restore a couple for new uses. But it's the history, standing or eroding, that entices Carol to walk around here and wonder about the people who knew this place before her.

Down the hill, closer to the creek, the Smiths have built a larger main house. Carol walks through it with pleasure and a little trepidation. She doesn't say it, but part of her still loves the Cozy Cabin best.

Opposite: When the inside of the cabin gets "too cozy," the open porch beckons with a well-set table and a little-seen angle of the Bridgers to the northeast.

A little bit of country style, courtesy of an antique farm table and a cupboard converted to a wet bar, combined with a touch of kitsch from a vintage sign sets the playful tone for the dining room and kitchen.

Opposite: The low ceilings in the living room create a comfy atmosphere that is enhanced by casual furnishings —a mix of old and new—and the colorful artwork of Edd Enders to brighten up the woodsy interior.

In the master bedroom, simplicity and bright colors prevail to create a warm, inviting respite.

In the children's bedroom, three wrought-iron beds covered with quilts, striped pillows, and cowboy-inspired accessories play on the cabin's bunkhouse roots.

A flower box at the top of the stairs frames views of the Bridger Mountain Range.

CHAPTER 2

# DOUBLE D RANCH

Photography by Gordon Gregory

Directions to the Double D Ranch read like a scavenger hunt: Turn right on "no name road"; drive past the old white farmstead; take left fork in the road; look for the cairn of boulders and keep driving up and up through rock tailings until you see the cabin. It's on 750 acres near McAllister, and like any authentic Montana ranch, it's not showy or large. Instead, it's full of inviting charm. When the front door opens, a sweet needlepoint sign greets the visitor: "To a friend's house the road is never long."

The evolution of Dick and Diana Beattie's Double D Ranch began with Dick's fervor for fly fishing. He spent enough time in Montana during the 1990s that the couple decided to find a property where they could relax over the summer months, away from New York City.

Diana knew what she wanted from the start— a great Adirondack camp out West—and went to work with Candace Tillotson-Miller of Miller Architects and Yellowstone Traditions to achieve it. She toured the state with Harry Howard, founder of Yellowstone Traditions, in search of reclaimed timber for the main house at the Double D. Eventually they found three historic log buildings, which were restacked on the Beatties' property.

Miller Architects and Yellowstone Traditions are noted for their meticulous attention to detail and have a well-earned reputation as a team that builds homes with incredible design, craftsmanship, and

Opposite: Yellowstone Traditions followed Diana Beattie's direction to "Twig it up!" by adorning the facade of the covered entry with branchwork that acts as a kind of rustic gingerbread trim.

In a space-saving measure, an L-shaped bar and shelf unit, faced with soldiered logs, separates the cooking area from the main living space.

sensitivity to place. Coupled with Diana's decisiveness, the main house was finished in ten months.

A large 1870s barn was restacked to make up the general living area, and two cabins were connected "dogtrot" style for the three bedrooms in the private side of the home. The covered entry is constructed of stone harvested from abandoned mines on the property, providing an appropriate nod to the regional roots. Another unique feature of the entrance is the fanciful twigwork under the gable, an ode to classic Adirondack embellishments and a true statement of Diana's personal style. She collected each piece of twisted wood, drew up the design, and gave Yellowstone Traditions' project manager, Justin Bolind, the directive "Twig it up!"

Opposite: A series of log trusses act as a structural and sculptural link in the open living, kitchen, and breakfast area.

Inside, through a casual vestibule, a washed palette of earth tones enhances the warmth and depth of the wood interior. Deep-set divided-light windows display views of the east end of the lower Madison Valley, framing the scenes like landscape paintings.

Back East, Diana runs her own firm, Diana Beattie Interiors, but only accepts a few clients a year. She is a passionate collector of antiques and classic rustic furnishings and has a deep appreciation of the intricate craftsmanship that grew out of the Adirondack style in the mid-1800s. Diana takes on design projects that engage her artistic sensibility and love of history, and her own home is a living museum of reverence for all things beautiful and intricate. She rattles off the names of the artisans who have created custom furnishings throughout the Double D's cluster of cabins, not to impress, but simply because she treasures every little detail.

Stepping down into the kitchen and living room

Whimsical details—such as the branchwork over the entry, the hand-glazed topographical maps in the powder room, and the many detailed Adirondack-style furnishings—were a way for the owners to personalize the main house. The result is true to historic cabin roots, in that everything in this home feels original, personal, handcrafted.

An authentic rustic touch is added to the house by utilizing a cut from the trunk of a massive Douglas fir as a stepway to the kitchen.

logs and a bookshelf to conceal the cook's work. The showpiece of the kitchen is a handcrafted pantry, replicated from a picture of a Russian hutch that Diana brought to Yellowstone Traditions' carpenters. It introduces the rich yellow and red motif that occurs throughout the house.

In the living area, the leather couches blend with the natural color scheme of the logs, remaining nearly "invisible" in order to showcase exquisite custom furniture like the unusual fly-tying desk by Adirondack artist Barney Bellinger set prominently against the far wall. The desk is made of cherry wood and pieces of bamboo from seventeen antique fly rods and features a handpainted trout at its crown. Whether hand-carved, painted, made from burled wood or reclaimed timbers, ever present in each work of art or piece of furniture is nature. Every element enhances the landscape outside, reducing human separation from it and drawing the outdoors in.

"I believe you should use products of nature— it's wood, it's leather, it's wool," Diana said, gesturing toward the comfortable living room setting in front of the stone fireplace. "I don't like to fight with nature."

A massive, solid wooden door leads to the back porch, where Old Hickory benches and chairs are

area, the wood wraps into a striking space, filled with original detail and character. Exposed log trusses add a sculptural focus to the room. The kitchen occupies a corner, efficiently built with a two-level, L-shaped counter that is decoratively wrapped with vertical

draped with 1930s Beacon blankets and a round Old Hickory table sits near the stepped-stone fireplace. The Beatties dine outside on the patio most nights in the summer.

Back inside, moving through a diamond-patterned pocket door to the private area of the house, there is a subtle shift in mood. The bedrooms are a refined version of cabin style, featuring luxuriously plastered walls to soften the woodsy interiors. Hand-hewn logs accent the muted color palette of the rooms, where Black Forest trophy mounts and European antiques are married with rustic pieces.

A narrow hallway leads to the guest suite, which was hand-troweled with spring green cat-eye plaster by Jennifer Besson. The room features a country bed from Milan and is accented with washed Kilim rugs, two Oriental carpets, and a 1750s French hutch. Flanking the guest room is the children's bunkroom, where cozy log beds are stacked to create a magical hideout. Tiny red cowboy boots are placed to the side of the bottom bunk, and a treasure trove of precious collectible toys call out to be played with.

A banister made of a latticework of shed-horn antlers leads upstairs to a secret retreat. Up here, in the "treetop room," goldenrod-colored linens draw out the hand-painted detail of an antique Brittany armoire. Diana defined each room with freestanding storage units, whose interiors she carefully lined with fabric, adding her own custom touch.

In the master bedroom, an elegant four-poster bed sets the tone for a romantic setting that looks out toward rolling hills and distant mountains. In the bedrooms, Diana allows more color and decoration to draw attention inside in order to focus on unwinding. A lavish bathroom with willow cabinetry

A richly colored, hand-painted hutch by Jennifer Besson conceals the pantry. The hutch was inspired by a Russian antique that Diana Beattie saw in a design book.

and fanciful twigwork beams echoes the woodwork of the front entry. Built-in closets, adorned with hand-applied willow work by David Black, repeat the diamond pattern that is a prevalent detail throughout the house.

The closet creates a passage that leads down a

curved stairway to Dick's office, where first editions of the best Western books line the shelves and adorn the walls, and sweeping views to the east facilitate his workday. A custom sideboard was scribed into stone along one side of the room, and craftsman David Latinen built a long, noble desk of white oak. The space overlooks a trail that leads down the hill to the trout pond.

During the summer months, when the flow of visiting friends and family is steady, the fishing soddie below the main house is the hub of activity. Nestled into the hillside, the small stone cabin is a bastion of rustic charm and a shady respite grounded with a sense of place. The stacked stones allude to the enchanting rough simplicity of the earliest homestead cabins that utilized the most available materials around. Waders and other angling gear remain at the ready in the soddie, which is located near the trout-stocked pond.

Extending the rambling atmosphere of a ranch compound is the Swedish guesthouse that the Beatties built nearby. It's a magical cabin, filled with such incredible artistry that it could be a living-history exhibit. Originally built by Swedish immigrants in 1912 and reconstructed here, the multilevel structure celebrates the settlement of the West.

The guesthouse's steep-gabled corrugated-metal roof is a classic design built to bear heavy snow loads. Intertwined twigs embellish the facade of the upper gable and the eave above the front door, where the ranch's brand—two mirror-image Ds— hangs. Draped with hop vines, the enchanting entry is only a precursor to the riches that can be found in this masterfully crafted cottage. The front door is an elaborate work of willow-twig art, while inside a

A diminutive fly-tying desk created by Adirondack furniture maker Barney Bellinger utilizes broken antique fly rods and features a hand-painted angling image.

Opposite: A refined rustic look was achieved by juxtaposing a willow-twig hutch featuring the house's signature diamond pattern and a carved Queen Anne detail at the top, created by Montana artisan David Black, against the dark, hand-peeled log walls.

On the back patio, an intimate round Old Hickory table overlooks the Madison Range in the distance. A bronze restrike of Charles Ramsey's sculpture *The Buffalo Hunt* brings a refined element to this setting.

hand-painted Scandinavian wedding scene by Jennifer Besson is the first hint of Diana's intrepid devotion to the art of the home.

Once a gold-mining placer, the property is now used by the Beatties to raise American paint horses that are considered to be some of the best stock in the country. Diana's favorite horses are housed in a barn that is appropriately constructed from another reclaimed and restacked log barn. The rustic simplicity of the main house continues even here, where the weathered logs and tin roof look as if they haven't changed for over a century.

"We didn't want to build a castle ranch in Big Sky country that dwarfed our surroundings," said Diana. "We wanted to build a place that was comfortable and people-sized." This the Beatties achieved, with beautifully understated buildings that foster a sense of history.

Opposite: Typical of the Adirondack style brought West, the low-slung porch is an integral outdoor living space with 1930s Old Hickory furnishings and the warmth of classic Beacon blankets.

18

Cat-eye hand-troweled plaster walls add a fresh luster to the log accents in the bedroom areas. Diana Beattie used bold colors in the bedrooms and placed European antiques in them to achieve a feeling of the classic homesteader's story of emigrating West.

Opposite: Tucked into the smallest room of the house, the children's bunkroom is adorned with cowboy kitsch and charming built-in beds crafted by Yellowstone Traditions.

Massive boulders were stacked to create this rustic cabin that resembles the most primitive structures in Ireland. The owners use it as a fun anglers' retreat to base a day casting into the trout pond for native browns.

Opposite: The stairs that descend to Dick Beattie's office were an addition to the master suite and hint at the curved elements of a tepee.

Antique creels add texture and visual interest.

A Swedish flag playfully flies at the guesthouse's front door, which is embellished by David Black's artistic bent-willow twigwork.

The Double D's Swedish guesthouse pays homage to the early roots of this region with its steep-pitch gabled roof and ornate trim details of rustic gnarled branches and burled wood.

Continuing the authentic Western style throughout the ranch, the barn is made of logs from a century-old barn reclaimed near Dillon, Montana, and restacked here.

## CHAPTER 3

# CANYON RESPITE

Photography by Roger Wade

A swath of farmland runs sweet and fertile in the shallow belly of Bridger Canyon before it is scooped up into the whittled peaks of southwest Montana's Bridger Range. A deep-cut creek ambles along the valley floor, nurturing hay and barley fields, cattle and horses. It runs under a wide-planked bridge, wending around a curve of cottonwoods past a house that exudes a romantic Western charm.

For Mark and Addie Theisen, building a home in Montana was all about comfort. Though a compromise would need to be found between his taste for clean-lined architecture and her yearning for a cozy log cabin, the couple agreed that the house should incorporate natural materials from the region and that it should be a complete departure from their primary residence in Florida. While driving around the area looking for ideas, they discovered the collection of historic National Park Service buildings near Yellowstone's Mammoth Hot Springs. Made of log and stone and featuring low-hanging eaves and big

windows, the bungalows seemed to capture a period of the West that appealed to the Theisens.

"I wanted a house that felt like it had been there a long time, that felt lived in, warm, and comfortable," Addie says. "We liked the Craftsman style and knew the wood and stone would blend easily into the landscape."

Mark was familiar with the Greene and Greene style of architecture so prominent in his native Southern California. With this style in mind, the Theisens began the design process with Jerry Locati, principal at Locati Architects in Bozeman.

At the entry, stacked Montana stone provides a sense of place, while the artistry of the Craftsman-style front door, custom-made Locati light fixture, and combination of building materials—including board and batten siding, cedar shingles, and timber-frame elements—signal that this is a very contemporary cabin that seamlessly melds the past and present.

The heart of this Locati-designed house lies in the use of natural elements: stone, wood, and light. From the great room, the view of the Bridgers changes throughout the day; likewise, the mood in the house shifts with the sunlight entering through the wall of windows facing the mountain range.

**Combining the cozy dimensions of a traditional cabin with the highly refined elements of the Craftsman style, Locati Architects created a new kind of retreat. Unlike the compact proportions of a small, dark log structure that was meant strictly as a shelter from the harsh mountain climate, the owners wanted a retreat that allowed them to appreciate their surroundings even when they were indoors. Vaulted ceilings add an expansive feeling to the great room and showcase the sculptural arched trusses. As a result, the succession of arches bridges the main portion of the house from the central kitchen out to the dining and living room and beyond to the outdoors.**

"Greene and Greene, as well as Frank Lloyd Wright and the Mission style, have been strong influences in my thought process, especially when I started out fifteen years ago," claims Locati. "They have the kind of details that make a house warm, like exposed beams and rafter tails, but also continuing structural details throughout the design to bring out stronger architectural elements."

In this case, Locati Architects managed to achieve a modern, regionalized bungalow branded with their own finesse. The result is a unique juxtaposition of massive Montana stone and wood with a refined nod to the Craftsman style. What prevails in the house is its perfect proportion and scale, customary in a cabin retreat.

At only 2,300 square feet, the house bursts with artful details that create seamless transitions from entryway to living room to kitchen to bedrooms.

Where Greene and Greene may have used teak or mahogany woods, Locati used native yellow pine, alder, and recycled fir. High ceilings and expansive windows keyed to views of the Bridgers lend openness without sacrificing intimacy.

Arguably the best example of the Locati team's ability to meld historic American architecture with modern living is the home's compact foyer. Stepping over the threshold, the entry is flooded with natural light filtered through the door's mullioned windows and a row of wheat-colored stained-glass windows along the upper wall. A custom-made iron light fixture accentuates the graceful pattern of the pressed-tin ceiling, and a wall of built-in cabinets neatly stores boots and coats. Near the doorway to the garage, a classic hanging desk acts as a catchall for car keys, cell phones, and mail. This is where the Craftsman influence is strongest, yet the slate floor hints at a contemporary component.

From the foyer the living room beckons. An immense stone fireplace dominates the far wall, anchored by a fifteen-foot-long single slab of stone that makes up the hearth bench. The living area is linked to the kitchen and enticing back porch by an open floor plan. Recycled-wood trusses establish the structural line of the house. Like vertebrae in a spine, four successive arches frame the living area, the rear deck, the creek, and ultimately the mountain view.

Just as true bungalows extolled the casual lifestyle of early twentieth-century California, so too does Locati's design here. In a relatively small space, the house exudes an air of relaxation that lends itself to Mark and Addie's love of nature.

While in Montana, the Theisens dabble in the things they love: fly fishing, tying flies, pottery, and

Earthy colors and furniture, along with Arts and Crafts–inspired light fixtures, enhance the natural materials of the stone fireplace and recycled fir trusses. The Arts and Crafts style was a way for the owners to combine their separate tastes in a way that celebrates simplicity, craftsmanship, and a reverence for the natural world.

woodworking. Just a short walk from their house, a small building near the classic old red barn serves as a studio for both of them. The property has become a family retreat, a place to forget Florida and tinker with the idea of living out here full time.

"I love every part of the house," Mark explains. "From the trout carvings on the exposed rafters, to the way the siding and shingles flow together, to the stained-glass windows."

Working with designer Donna Brooks, of

Compact and functional, the kitchen is where the master craftsmanship of Mountain High Woodworks shines through, with alder cabinetry that echoes the square panes of the house's true-divided-light windows.

Brooks Interior Design in Florida, the Theisens made the house their own. Brooks helped Addie choose the earthy color scheme and shopped in Santa Fe, New Mexico, and California for furnishings. As a result, the color of plaster in each room of the house resembles the dark, secretive hues of river rocks—deep browns and greens. The Arts and Crafts–style light fixtures mirror the warm motif of Montana sunrises.

The expert level of craftsmanship is evident in

the detailed woodwork in every room of the house. In the kitchen, the cabinetry perfectly links the breakfast nook; in the master bedroom, the built-in closets actually create a woodsy atmosphere in the dressing area, bringing the warm feel of a forest to the room. Even in the master bath, where a wall of cabinets frames the vanity and travertine countertop, the space feels larger than it actually is. The built-in features also help keep clutter hidden.

Ultimately, the Theisens and Locati Architects managed to blend elements of those rustic structures in Yellowstone with the sophisticated California bungalow style to create an elegant, unobtrusive, and practical living space in Montana.

The Montana stone fireplace adorned with a hand-forged fire screen serves as the focal point of the living room.

The master bedroom on the upper level is simple and tasteful, with the warm glow from nearby hayfields shining through the window. A small, private sitting area takes advantage of the morning light.

Montana travertine lines the counter of the double vanity in the master bath. Custom-made Locati light fixtures add exquisite detail to the simple space that is a private haven with a soaking tub, steam shower, and radiant heat floors.

An inviting deck faces the nearby creek and the Bridger Range to the northeast. The exposed rafter tails and dominant arch carry the structural and aesthetic weight of the house, extending the interior living space through the French doors to a covered porch.

CHAPTER 4

# CELEBRATING THE BARN

Photography by Tom Ferris

Up a dusty farm road in Montana's Gallatin Valley, a classic red barn sits on a hill. Its roof slopes and peaks with the mountains around it. The trotting horse weather vane that sits atop the cupola is still, pointing southeast, and the hand-blown glass lightning rods catch morning sunlight. From a distance it appears like any other old barn—functional and formidable—but a closer look reveals the structure's new purpose as a home for people rather than livestock.

The owners rescued the building from demolition in nearby Paradise Valley. It was the last structure to be sold at a ranch cleanup, having been rejected by local salvage businesses who sell reclaimed wood structures to builders and architects. The price tag on the barn was $500, and the current owners figured the antique cupola alone was worth at least that. They arranged for the barn to be moved one valley over, 23 miles to the west, across a mountain pass and over the winding farm roads on either side.

"This is sort of the vernacular of Montana," said the husband, a former architect from California. "It's more at home here than anything we could have built."

**Opposite: The owners found a way to reuse most of the structure's materials, including the trotting horse weathervane.**

**Overleaf: According to architect Thor Arnold, the goal was to save the character of the barn on the outside while adapting it for multiple needs inside and making it as energy efficient as possible.**

Crafting an open floor plan from what was once a dairy barn is a challenge, but the kitchen, living, and dining areas blend into one seamlessly inviting space.

Like a classic homesteader's cabin, this reclaimed barn was sited for easy access to the road, in a sunny location to absorb passive solar benefits, and in a curve of land that provides protection from prevailing winds. Architect Thor Arnold was also careful to honor the agricultural roots of the gambrel-roofed structure, adding Montana stone on the building's main level and setting it into the hillside.

Working with Bozeman architect Thor Arnold of zimtor architecture and general contractor Clay Bowden of Livingston, the couple embarked on a serendipitous experience. They chose the building for its elegant shape and connection to the land, but soon realized that renovating a barn is no simple task.

"From the beginning this barn has had a life of its own," said the wife. "This house is a living thing. It has its own spirit."

Like a historic cabin, the building reflected Montana's rich past. Converting the barn into a home presented challenges in design and construction, making the process take longer than a new house, but the result is truly original. The footprint of the building largely dictated the layout of living spaces, and the site dictated the barn's orientation toward the sun and views and away from prevailing winds.

"We wanted to honor the building and where it came from," recalled architect Arnold, "so at least in form and volume the barn is true to its roots."

The gambrel roof is typical of structures built in the northern United States between 1900 and 1940. Though its intent was purely utilitarian—to maximize the size of the hayloft above the dairy

Much like a cabin, the kitchen's hearth is the anchor of the barn house. A high counter is made of a large plank that was once part of the floor in the bull stall. The owners also reclaimed original windows from the barn in order to reuse them in custom cabinets crafted by McPhie Cabinetry.

—the shape has become the iconic image of an American barn.

After World War II, when mechanical balers made it more practical to store hay outside, most new farm outbuildings were single-story and constructed of galvanized metal or plywood. Honoring this architectural vernacular, Arnold designed a shed-style garage clad in corrugated steel and attached it to the main house with a cabin-inspired breezeway.

From the outside, the different materials incor-porated into the main house, garage, and breezeway are an attractive example of the reclamation of the barn as a residence. The industrial element of steel on the garage is softened by warm reclaimed barn-wood planks, applied vertically and running into the dry-stack stone at the base of the home, which then segues upward to the original clapboard siding on the upper level. The effect flows in the same way that years pass—one into another—with time and lines blending into a whole experience.

"The goal was to save the character of this barn on the outside—its thin roofline, exposed rafter tails, and wood siding—while adapting it for multiple needs inside and making it as energy efficient as possible," said Arnold.

To reinforce and adapt the ground floor of the structure, Arnold designed a new foundation and surrounded it with sustainable Durisol insulated wood concrete forms. On the exterior, stone was stacked against the blocks, and on the interior walls, plaster was troweled over the raw material.

Inside, the character of the building remains, with the natural wood tones of the hewn beams educing the warmth of a cabin. Stepping into the main living area, warm light softly filters through the windowpanes the way it does inside a barn. Of course, the space has been updated for comfortable modern living, but elements of the barn remain. Its original metal sliding-door tracks have been utilized to hang new doors made of wood from the old building. It's not a stretch to imagine stalls between the hand-hewn posts that support the structure, keeping the room open and airy without dividing walls.

The owners tried to save everything they could from the original building and reuse it in a different way. They compiled an album of snapshots to record the "before and after" of the barn, cataloging the dilapidated wood, peeling red paint, and interesting hooks and hardware that came with it. Even the hay hook and pulley system that hung outside the loft upstairs was saved; it sits, curiously sculptural, on the front porch.

In the kitchen, custom-built cabinets incorporate more barn wood, pulled from old stalls and planed to bring out a variety of color and grain. The upper glass cupboards display china cups, plates, and wine glasses; the frames are made from the barn's original windows. The husband labored meticulously to make the frames true and square again in order to function in their new form, and McPhie Cabinetry of Bozeman completed the task and installed the cabinets. A thick plank that was once part of the bull stall was used for the counter, where a trio of stools now sit. Granite countertops coupled with a traditional white porcelain farm sink also blend new and old.

The contemporary open floor plan effortlessly links the cooking, dining, and living areas. The thick walls are layered with a milky-colored plaster, maximizing the attention drawn to the outside views—each one like a landscape painting. An acid-stained amber-speckled concrete floor is a modernist nod, with a utilitarian link that is not far from the barn's line. Down the hall, a bedroom, lavish bathroom, and laundry room are located in the private portion of the house, which is set into the hillside.

Back in the main room, a Tulikivi soapstone wood-burning stove is the focal point and one of the couple's favorite amenities. It efficiently heats the house and anchors the living area in its own right. Beside the stove, a staircase leads up to the loft, where the bones of the barn open up. This vast space cried out to be left as it was when it stored the hay. Arnold added skylights and slightly larger windows on both sides of the loft, but kept the stick frame trusses exposed.

A library wraps around the center of the loft, which also contains a master suite on one end and the couple's painting and working studio on the opposite end. The vastness of the space was a conundrum when it came to converting it for practical living,

Incorporating low-maintenance regional materials is a trademark of zimtor architecture. The ground floor of the house is insulated with Durasil blocks beneath the stacked Harlowton stone on the outside and smoothed with a creamy milk-white plaster on the walls inside.

but the interior design team at Montana Expressions cleverly divided it into three practical areas to create privacy without walls. Using well-placed furnishings that echo an eclectic old-world, rustic style, the designers successfully created interior vignettes for the bedroom, library, and studio. Between the library and bedroom, a tall custom-built armoire utilizes corrugated metal and barn wood to connect with the architectural language of the house. On the other end of the library, a freestanding screen, made of more aged steel and an old barn window, creates privacy around the studio/office space.

Remembering advice from her mother, who once said that every view inside your house should be a still life, the wife has carefully placed her art collection, books, and treasured objects throughout the home. As a result, at nearly every turn there is an artful display that highlights the thoughtful design that has gone into making this home so unique.

Both of the owners sigh with memories of the frustration they felt time and again during the finishing of their barn house. Unlike new construction, nothing in this house could be purchased out of the showroom or off the rack or shelf; instead, everything was custom-made to fit the unusual pitch of the roof, the unlikely style that the building naturally projected, or the openness of the space. The husband pored through salvaged barn wood and designed many of the pieces within the house himself, planing boards and finishing metal, even fabricating light fixtures and drawer pulls. But in the end, both knew they had a house like no other and it was worth the effort.

"It's been a long process, a creative process that doesn't happen fast—we had to let the barn speak to us," said the husband.

The soapstone masonry heater, constructed by WarmStone Fireplaces and Designs, is a contemporary centerpiece in the house.

Standing on the hill as a reminder of this valley's agricultural roots, the barn will always whisper of its past life, but what it says most now is: *come home.*

Upstairs, the former hayloft was converted into a living and sleeping space. The owners worked with the interior designer, Montana Expressions, to define the vast space without making it feel confining. To this end, the design team utilized freestanding room dividers constructed of corrugated metal and aged barn wood.

Custom-made wardrobes double as room dividers to create privacy for the master bedroom.

The library acts as a transition area between the privacy of the bedroom and the shared office space. Built-in barn-wood shelves line the wall, and an antique Spanish table anchors the area.

The owners consciously create still-life arrangements in every available space throughout the home.

**Opposite: A claw-foot bathtub, antique cupboard, crystal chandelier, and old family photo add a sense of romantic vintage style to the upstairs bathroom.**

## CHAPTER 5

# SPRINGHILL HIDEOUT

Photography by Roger Wade

Drive north out of Bozeman onto Springhill Road until the haystacks outnumber houses and the blonde-grass hills surround you. Turn right on an old dirt road and head toward the mountains of the Bridger Range. Take it slow, and look around and try to imagine when this valley was all farmland. Turn left, then right, and follow the old ranch road a mile or so until it starts to climb. You're heading into the mountains now, winding up until it feels as though you can drive right along "The Saddle" on the Bridger ridge and onto the western side of Ross Peak.

Crest the hill and you'll find a simple house sitting serenely in a mature aspen grove. At a glance it's hard to judge how old the place is, but a closer look tells you that the weathered wood siding has been re-crafted and assembled into a luxurious form. Designed by Locati Architects, it is an exquisite combination of historic Montana and modern living. Detail is a hall-

**Opposite: Locati Architects used hundred-year-old logs at the house's entrance to make a statement about this land's log cabin beginnings. Traditional chinking in the logs and heavy timbers on the porch speak of the classic architecture that remains strong in contemporary design today.**

mark of Jerry Locati's Bozeman firm, which is noted for incorporating reclaimed woods and native stone into intricate designs. Every inch of this 3,200-square-foot guest cabin is filled with custom features.

"The owner wanted this to be a showcase for Montana craftsmen," said project architect Kyle Tage, and indeed it is. A formidable list of artisans contributed to this home that is a tribute to Montana vernacular, with just about every conceivable contemporary luxury inside. The owner wanted to utilize existing structures on the ranch property to create a rustic retreat. The house is made from a hundred-year-old farm building that was moved and restacked for the

**In a remarkable effort to pay respect to the history of this property in southwest Montana, the owners requested that Locati Architects salvage several original, dilapidated homestead structures that remained on the land and recycle them into a new guest cabin. The outcome is an acute departure from the rustic cabins that once sheltered settlers here, but what remains is the patina absorbed by the wood—the product of the sun, wind, snow, and rain that faded the boards through the decades and now frame an entirely different vision of this fertile valley. Angled toward vast views of the west, this 3,200-square-foot home honors Montana vernacular without compromising modern luxury.**

exterior structure, using a combination of chinked log with board and batten. Thick cedar shingles line the roof, solid-bronze-clad Italian windows sink into the rough wood siding, and elaborate stacked stone columns mark the entrance of the house. Elegant, hand-made iron-and-glass light fixtures on the threshold belie the home's rustic simplicity.

Open the massive antique wood door to enter a room filled with handcrafted opulence. Wheat-tinted plaster walls offset the heavy structural detail of the arched wooden trusses and the massive stone fireplace with its wrought-iron mantle. The room engulfs you with a sheltering sophistication.

"My favorite feature of this project is how we used the old grain-storage building as part of the structure of the house," muses Locati. "The exterior has the look of an agricultural building with the old restack, but the interior has a refined look—it was a challenge to pull those two looks together."

The result is a dreamy cabin featuring old-world-quality craftsmanship. An open floor plan links the living room, kitchen, and dining areas, yet each space has its own feeling of intimacy. The kitchen is outfitted with professional-grade appliances, custom cabinets, marble countertops, and copper sinks. A breakfast nook wraps around a superb round oak table built by Richard Garwood's Mountain High Woodworks.

Continuing the language of an agricultural structure, a wrought-iron ladder climbs to the loft above the kitchen, where a study and media room are enclosed with an unusual iron railing handmade by local blacksmith Bill Moore. The best views of Ross Peak can be had from this cozy space, decorated with rich red and gold earth tones that bring the hues of the surrounding landscape into the home.

Back down the ladder, recycled antique Spanish oak floors spread a warm hue to each room in the house with accents of fir, ironwork, and stone. The walls are adorned with original paintings by local artists, including Rocky Hawkins, and several depict Yellowstone landscapes. Down the hall, a door with an abstract stained-glass window by David Fjeld opens to the lavish bathroom, which contains twin sinks and a tempting claw-foot tub. In the guest

**Opposite: Even a passageway in the cabin is highly detailed, showcasing Italian solid-bronze-clad windows in the jogged stone, juxtaposed with the repetition of clean lines formed by the metal and wood banister, the lantern lights, and the reclaimed wood beams.**

A long plank of thick aged wood centers the small but highly functional kitchen. Copper sinks, professional-grade appliances, and granite countertops are modern amenities that clearly depart from the rusticity of the early cabin days.

room, a handcrafted barn-wood bed frame and more mountain views ground the room.

A playful kids' room features six built-in bunk beds and another bathroom. Whimsical tile work plays on the theme of wildlife, with a colorful mosaic featuring a trout-filled creek and grizzly bears, and

Opposite: A heavy, antique wood door opens to a room filled with warmth and sophistication. The handcrafted opulence is evident immediately: the sculptural Harlowton stone fireplace and its forged iron mantle by Bill Moore, the arched timbers that form the high ceilings, the intricate ironwork ladder that leads to a loft overhead. Each element has leanings to the property's agricultural beginnings, but with an entirely contemporary application.

hand-painted rainbow trout in the sinks and swimming around the vanity.

Across the hall is the master bedroom, private and subdued on the lower level, with its own terrace overlooking a cool stand of aspens and a creek. Another decadent bathroom featuring tumbled Italian marble and a custom vanity flanks the room. A wall of rustic-looking built-in cabinets offers ample clothing and storage space, but it's the custom-designed wood and hammered steel bed that anchors the room.

The interior design was artfully pulled together by Locati Interiors. Missing are the hand-me-downs of traditional cabins, but still here is the connection to place—past and present.

The guest cabin is a showcase for regional artisans, whose custom-designed elements are incorporated into every corner of the structure. A local blacksmith fabricated the back stairway.

Outside, a porch leads from the house to a terrace that overlooks the vast stretches of farmland in the Gallatin Valley. A Viking grill is built into the stone wall surrounding the terrace, which is furnished with inviting, comfortable chairs. Below, in the aspens, a footpath beckons you to enjoy the dappled light and the tranquility that surrounds the cabin.

Opposite: Conserving space in the cabin tradition, the breakfast nook wraps around a hearty oak table constructed by Mountain High Woodworks. Flooded with early morning light from the east, the dining area draws in intimate views of the Bridgers.

Locati Architects designed the hammered steel and wood bed and had it constructed by Mountain High Woodworks to anchor the master suite.

The wrought-iron mantle and fireplace screen were made by Bill Moore. In the background, a row of bead-board doors on the closet echo the simple construction and materials typically used by homesteaders a century ago.

A stained-glass window by David Fjeld adds an elegant touch to the door leading into a luxurious bathroom. Sandstone-colored hand-troweled plaster on the walls sets the soothing tone of the space, which features an oversize cast-iron tub tucked into a timbered corner.

The outdoor living space is defined by architecturally applied stone that carves out a patio warmed by the sun throughout the day. Overstuffed cushions on round-back willow chairs invite lounging, while a hot tub sunken into the elaborate rockscape tempts a long soak. Just off the edge of the patio, a trail beckons hikers to explore a nearby aspen grove.

CHAPTER 6

# BIG SKY CABIN

Photography by Gordon Gregory

It isn't easy to get an invitation to interior designer Carole Sisson's weekend home. She and her husband, Gary, are protective of their private cabin south of Big Sky: It's the place where they don fuzzy slippers and while away spring days waiting for the nuthatches to visit a bird feeder outside their window. They read and cook and snowshoe—all the things they have no time to do during their usual harried workweek.

"We just fell in love with the land and the views," says Carol.

Both the pace of life and the architectural style of the home are a world away from the Sissons' primary residence in Bozeman. "Our house in town is more formal and much more traditional than this home," Carole explains. "We wanted the cabin to be a departure—something open, rustic, and easy to care for."

Nestled into the hillside at an elevation of 7,500 feet and bordering two million acres of national forest, the Sissons also felt it was important to build a house that fit into the landscape. They worked with Faure Halvorsen Architects in Bozeman and chose an eclectic blend of recycled wood and natural materials. The two-story home is constructed primarily of square-cut tamarack logs, reminiscent of a simple homestead cabin. With a nod to the area's agricultural roots, the attached garage utilizes doors from an old

red barn, and other weathered pieces of barn wood offset the logs. The eaves of a rusted corrugated-metal roof hang over whimsical pine-branch detailing that echoes gingerbread on a Victorian farmhouse.

Inside, many of the same reclaimed materials have been incorporated into the cabin's rectangular

The owners wanted to be part of the building process, so they walked the property to site the house at just the right angle toward Lone Peak and western views. They cleared the building site and collected wood to be incorporated into the decorative branching on the face of the house. Coming here is like a return to the land for them, especially since they were involved in every phase of construction.

A wicker chair adds a delicate touch that contrasts with the heavy slate, wide hand-adzed logs, and pine-branched railing at the front entry.

floor plan. Extra-wide sugar-pine plank floors span the main level of the house, where the great room and open kitchen turn toward spectacular mountain views. Warm maize-colored plaster walls enhance the layers of texture that envelope the senses like a soft blanket.

Native American artwork sets the tone for a contemporary Western motif that is interspersed with Carole's antique furniture and collectibles. Hand-adzed logs and chinking on the walls add contrasting texture to the rich fabrics used in window coverings and upholstery. High ceilings with exposed timbers give the main part of the house an expansive feel without being cavernous.

"The priority for their house was to create a livable space rather than a big show palace," recalls architect Kipp Halvorsen. "What they wanted to do was be more true to Montana vernacular by using rusticated material."

Although Carole claims the 4,000-square-foot home is a work-in-progress, it is expertly finished. Countless custom-made pieces from local artisans amplify the detail of the house. From the massive round dining room table, to the rich red marble-dusted paint in the powder room, to the clever headboard and shelving unit in the master bedroom, the Sissons' home has been thoughtfully personalized.

But the couple didn't rely completely on master craftspeople to build their dream cabin. Under the direction of general contractor Pat Johnson, they were involved in every aspect of construction. They cleared the building site themselves on weekends for two years, sleeping in a camper. Carole and Gary treated the exterior logs with ash and poured

the tinted cement floor in the basement. They even collected all the branches for the elaborate pine railing that frames the loft and lines the staircases. It was a chance to create something all their own and to experiment with some design concepts, but more than anything, it was a place for the Sissons to relax, be with family, and entertain close friends.

Time spent at the cabin means time spent in the great room and kitchen area, which anchors the house. The triangular kitchen is modestly sized but highly functional. It flows into the living and dining area, and sports tumbled slate countertops that echo the stone in the cliff behind the house. Sandblasted fir cabinets display hand-blown Italian glasses as well as colorful Tuscan-inspired dinnerware. Comfortable stools line the counter opposite the cooktop bringing guests into the kitchen action and offering a casual place to dine. Tasteful custom lighting throughout the kitchen effectively creates individual spaces despite the open floor plan.

Without question, the custom details in this secluded retreat are notable. Yet it's the quirky personal effects that give the house most of its character, like Gary's worn-looking reading chair in the loft, or Carole's funky thrift-shop chandelier over the soaking tub in the master bathroom. The rough, old-growth trees that frame the kitchen were salvaged from the property by the Sissons while clearing deadfall for the building site, and Carole found places for the enchanting color-washed Turkish doors she bought over a decade ago and the classic 1920s cook stove.

When the couple's grandchildren visit, they play chess and card games in the loft. It's cozy family activites like these, along with the satisfaction of having helped build the cabin, that Carole and Gary find most rewarding.

Opposite: Classic antiques add an eclectic style to the rustic cabin's hall.

The triangular kitchen is dominated by a comfortable bar framed with rough log pillars and high twigged stools.

The luxurious textures of the upholstery contrast with the rough hand-adzed logs and chinking in the great room, where owner Carole Sisson combined contemporary furnishings with her antiques collection.

Rustic log accents link the cabin to its mountain setting.

Opposite: A massive round table looks out onto the yard,
which is frequented by songbirds and other wildlife.

The use of more refined woods for the sleek and stylish bathroom achieved a spa-like atmosphere.

A custom-designed bed and shelf from Diane Cole Ross of Rustic Furniture in Montana combines a space-saving feature with a twig appliqué that reinforces the log elements throughout the house.

Faure Halvorsen Architects incorporated a blend of recycled wood and natural materials, using mostly square-cut tamarack logs, barn wood, and corrugated metal.

Opposite: Nestled into a hillside at 7,500 feet, this classic Big Sky cabin is surrounded by national forest.

CHAPTER 7

# COW CAMP STYLE

Photography by Gordon Gregory

It took a decade to find the property that Mike and Amy Bennett envisioned: a classic little log building not unlike the trailside museum at the confluence of the Madison and Gibbon Rivers in Yellowstone National Park, with a little stream out back, a meadow, and lots of trees. Mike would know it when he saw it, he told his friend and fishing guide, Randy Cain. Then one day, driving along the old gravel road on the east end of Ennis Lake, he spotted his cabin through the trees.

They turned into the driveway to get a closer look. The place wasn't for sale, but Bennett was smitten with it and eventually negotiated a deal with owner Jack Watkins Jr., a third-generation rancher.

"There was a lifetime accumulation of stuff that a typical rancher would collect, but I could see that the bones of the building were in incredible shape, and I thought it was gorgeous," recalls Mike.

**Opposite: Century-old hand-peeled logs with long "beaver tail" ends create a sculptural artistry within their rigid stacking.**

During the negotiation of the property, the Bennetts learned about the rich history of Watkins Creek Ranch. The Watkins family was one of the first to raise cattle in the Madison Valley in the late 1800s. The main house was constructed in 1906 by Jack Watkins Sr., who was a chief carpenter in the construction of Yellowstone's Old Faithful Inn. He applied the skills and artistry he'd learned on the job to his own family cabin, for which he harvested long, straight lodgepole pines and carefully stacked and chinked them to create a humble, but thoughtful, abode.

Flagstone paths connect each of the "camp" buildings, which are centered on the main house, built in 1906 by Jack Watkins Sr., a chief carpenter at the Old Faithful Inn in Yellowstone National Park.

Historically, several buildings were assembled in a compound to serve the multiple functions of a working cattle ranch. Rather than build one large house, it was customary to add smaller structures as needed for more sleeping quarters, storage, or shelter for animals. In this cow camp's transformation, the buildings remain to scale, but are clustered slightly closer than the original ranch plan. And they are used slightly differently—for entertaining guests, relaxing, or just plain fun.

In classic cow camp style, smaller cabins were added to accommodate ranch hands, storage, and livestock, and it was these outbuildings that sparked Mike's interest in creating a ranch compound. Shortly after he acquired the property, he began interviewing architects and contractors to restore the main house. A developer and contractor in his home state of South Carolina, Mike had been restoring historic buildings in Charleston for nearly thirty years

Ultimately, Mike chose to work with Candace Tillotson-Miller of Miller Architects and Harry Howard of Yellowstone Traditions. "I think they both really appreciated the house," he says. "Rather than say, 'It's an old house that needs a lot of work,' they said, 'This is a rare find.' It's a charming old building and it needs some tender, loving care."

Mike wanted to create a ranch compound with a series of small buildings rather than one grand mansion. Miller helped finesse the concept, and the work began. The road was rerouted, the classic weathered buildings were relocated closer to the main house, and the property, which was overgrown and

"All of us were so endeared by the scale and detail of the house," explains Miller. "It's this kind of elegance and intimacy that we try to replicate in new projects."

Miller quickly realized that there was much more to the property than the main house, such as the walkway through the century-old lilac hedge, the shade of the towering cedars, and the sense of shelter that the land offers with its natural configuration in a drainage of the Madison Range. And then there is the broad view across the hayfield toward Ennis Lake and the ever-present sound of Watkins Creek. She wanted to piece each ingredient together to make the ranch complex feel more diminutive and less industrial.

One way Miller accomplished this was to change the approach to the house from the main road, rerouting it to amble along a stand of cottonwoods, concealing the house until the final crossing over an irrigation ditch into the driveway. She added front and back porches to the main house, along with French doors to accommodate indoor-outdoor living. Yellowstone Traditions built the extensions, carefully matching the newly added log to the original structure, which features dovetailed corners with "beaver tail" log ends.

Inside, the overall floor plan of the 2,000-square-foot home had an open flow, and the condition of the logs was remarkable. To lighten up the dark interior, Miller added taller, deeper windows to replace the

neglected, was cleared of junk, including thirty-one abandoned Cadillacs.

Miller inventoried the existing elements of the main house and outlying buildings and then carefully enhanced them. Working with Howard and Yellowstone Traditions, she was confident that the sensitivity for the historic quality of the project would be a priority.

80

original "matchbox" ones. The kitchen, which had been home to a multitude of cats, was reclaimed and modernized. But on the whole, Miller's approach was to "land lightly" and work with the amenities that already existed within the historic cabin.

Interior designer Diana Beattie, of Diana Beattie Interiors, New York, outfitted Watkins Creek Ranch as though it were her own. Mike Bennett approached her to complete the interiors within a few weeks, with the directive, "Make it look like Teddy Roosevelt lived here." Beattie, whose expertise is in embellishing a traditional rustic style for contemporary living, rose to the challenge. Relying on her long-term supplier relationships and connections with local artisans for custom furnishings, and incorporating pieces from her own collection of 1930s handmade Old Hickory furniture, Beattie drew on her passion for the Adirondack camp style. She crafted elegant living spaces that masterfully complement the time and place of this home, using a natural palette of color to allow the structural beauty of the log cabin to stand out.

In the great room, the original elements of the home steal the scene: the twisted juniper banister that leads upstairs to a loft; the white quartzite fireplace made from stones found on the property; the dramatic pendant light that showcases three bighorn sheep harvested by the original owner. Rather than challenge these unique elements, Beattie enhanced

Opposite: Borrowing designs from Yellowstone's Old Faithful Inn, the twisted juniper banister offers intriguing contrast to the rigid symmetry of the log walls. The turned legs of an antique Italian sideboard echo the burled spiral of the juniper balusters.

their presence by placing furnishings with a subtle hand.

She combined classic rustic pieces with antiques to echo the era when the home was built, a time when homesteaders typically had a few stand-out family heirlooms in addition to their simple furnishings. An antique Swedish chest was placed between the leather furniture, a Black Forest breakfront sits in the corner, and an intricate round Adirondack table supports a reading lamp—each bringing a personalized eclecticism to the room. Kilim rugs add a jolt of color to the woodsy brown scheme, and original paintings by regional artists punctuate the sense of place in the cabin. Also key to the interior design was Beattie's ability to blend masterfully crafted furnishings by artisan David Black and lighting created by "Fish" Fisher of Fish Antler Art.

The three bedrooms are tucked down the hall from the main living space, each decorated with brightly colored linens and well-placed handmade furniture. In the master bedroom, Black crafted an intricate willow-twig headboard with carvings by Jans Carlsen: a trout swimming on award-winning angler Amy's side, and a bevy of quail on bird hunter Mike's side. Bringing in the work of contemporary artists was a way of honoring the original craftsmanship of this historic home, and it was an essential element in connecting the compound's separate buildings.

Back outside, a path leads from the back door to extended living spaces along the creek. Thoughtful landscape design, flagstone paths, and perennial plantings link the different structures.

Over the bridge is the smoking room, carved into the hillside by the original owner like a bunker.

An arched opening was cut into the logs and trimmed out, separating the dining room from the living room. The architect added deep, tall windows to provide light to offset the darkness of the log walls.

Two creations by the original owner—a living room chandelier showcasing the mountain sheep he harvested shortly after building the cabin and a white quartzite fireplace made of stone quarried on the property—stand as some of the unique customized elements in this unusual Western cabin.

Miller called upon master blacksmith Bill Moore to craft an arched metal and glass door for the space, which houses a custom billiard table and accommodates outdoor dining on the terrace.

In the other direction, the path leads to the cozy fishing cabin. The restacked log cabin is a departure from the main house, in that the huge, many-paned window looks directly toward the lake. Yet the simple style of the cabin is in line with the "Parkitec-ture" influence that exists throughout the property. Waders hang outside on the small porch. Inside, an Adirondack-style twigged fly-tying desk is the central focus and activity for this creekside structure.

Farther up the creek is a building that resembles a traditional bunkhouse. It's the Dog Trot—two original cabins that were reclaimed, relocated here, and connected by a single porch. Used as guest quarters, each cabin has one bedroom, a private bath, and

The small dining area features 1930s Old Hickory caned chairs and a shed-horn chandelier by Fish Fisher.

kitchen facilities. Vintage oil lanterns decorate the exterior logs under the covered porch, where stairs on the backside lead to a flagstone fire pit along the creek. Inside, spare but tasteful rustic furnishings and kitschy camp art continue the playful, historic Western style.

Furthering the cow camp concept of connectivity, the Bennetts extended the ranch property to include Ennis Lake, with an outdoor pavilion and boathouse in progress down at the lakeshore. They also plan to enhance the outdoor dining area for summer gatherings by converting an old woodshed into a custom kitchen for entertaining. Miller notes that while the compound allows the Bennetts privacy, it also provides the family with the ability to get together in a variety of spaces, moving from one building to another and utilizing the entire property. In the long run, the idea is to remain close to home.

The kitchen was rebuilt by Yellowstone Traditions' craftsmen, proving designs of the past can be replicated with equal artistry today.

This child's bedroom proudly features artisan woodworker David Black's Adirondack-style willow-twig headboards, which the interior designer enhanced with a strong crayon color scheme of fabrics.

The master bedroom may not be grand, but luxurious layers of bed linens add dimension to the small space with color that enhances the dark brown motif.

The mudroom was added to give this fly-fishing couple ample room to hang their angling gear.

The fishing cabin sits along Watkins Creek, down a short footpath from the main house. Constructed from an original outbuilding on the property, it was disassembled, restacked, and re-chinked on this site to unite the flow of activity around the reconfigured compound.

In the corner of the small fishing cabin, a jeweler's desk embellished with elk-horn drawer pulls, willow-twig monogramming, and hand-painted designs made by Adirondack artist Barney Bellinger, stands in as a functional fly-tying desk.

Opposite: Through a mullioned glass door, dropped kingpin trusses draw the eye to the "bones" of the cabin, which are simple but beautiful.

Formerly a welder's shop or some kind of machine shop, the owners converted this unique space into a billiards room. The riveted metal ceiling is original and curves with the contour of the hillside above. The architect reclaimed the space by pouring a concrete floor and adding a dramatic set of steel-and-glass doors made by blacksmith Bill Moore of Big Timber. The shop is situated across the creek from the main house and is now fronted by a flagstone patio that is the perfect spot for evening cocktails when the summer sun is setting.

Architect Candace Tillotson-Miller gracefully connected two of the property's original cabins with a breezeway, or "dogtrot" porch, which draws the eye to the plain structures that could as easily be a bunkhouse for cowhands as a posh guesthouse for the owners' friends and family. On the other side of the breezeway, an outdoor fire pit is an inviting creekside getaway.

Inside each guest cabin are two double beds covered with cozy down comforters and old Beacon blankets. Campy cabin art sets the playful tone of the space.

## CHAPTER 8

# VINTAGE CHARM

Photography by Roger Wade

At the end of a fir-lined road, far from the summer bustle of Bigfork, Montana, is a family retreat with old-world charm. It is marked only by a woodchip of a sign with the house number scrawled on it, nailed to a tree at the entrance of the driveway. Made of hand-hewn logs and reclaimed timbers, the house is as subdued as the breeze in the treetops that tower above it.

The owners discovered the property in the winter, trudging through knee-high snow into this meadow on an overcast day. The real estate agent promised that there would be amazing mountain views when the weather cleared, and the couple bought the property on her word. Construction began the following summer in the meadow, oriented toward the actual view of the distant Swan Range mountains, with architect Joe Magaddino of Bigfork teaming up with Denman Construction.

"We started with the concept of building an old ranch house that was cobbled together over the years," said Magaddino. "We wanted it to look old, like something the owner's great-grandfather might have built here."

The low-slung covered porch at the home's entrance speaks of an era with a slower pace. Inside, a series of high windows in the great room offer a floor-to-ceiling view of the mountains, and a massive native-rock fireplace tumbles into the central seating area. Hand-troweled, buckskin-colored plaster walls complement the high-style leather sofa and chairs, along with the earth-toned accessories.

Opposite: To brighten the neutral brown of the hewn logs, the owner selected a complementary green paint to trim the windows and the fascia. The back porch overlooks the Swan Range and beckons with an assortment of handmade Amish rocking chairs.

Inspired by the look and feel of traditional homesteader materials, the owners built their own interpretation of a cabin in the woods. The house is tucked into a forest of aspens and Douglas firs, and incorporates hewn logs, square timbers, reclaimed barn wood, stone accents, and a touch of old-world charm. With the Swan Range mountains in the distance and a creek running through the property, the house embodies a sense of seclusion that is uncommon in modern retreats. In that way, the owners have re-created the privacy that an old log cabin might have had long ago, but they've also incorporated all the modern necessities under one roof, with space for guests, entertainment, cooking, art, and work.

Tucked two steps above the great room is the dining room, a delightful departure from the typical rustic mountain home. The ceiling lowers intimately, and a stout-legged harvest table dominates the cozy hearth that resembles those found in French country cottages, with staggered bricks and a low-hanging trio of lanterns.

The owner, who is an artist and interior designer, said she wanted the house to look as though it was homesteaded by European immigrants who adapted family heirlooms to a new way of life. Her fanciful approach influenced Magaddino's creativity in custom details throughout the home.

Just off the dining room, a butler's pantry leads to a well-crafted kitchen, where the brickwork continues around a more contemporary hearth that encircles the professional-grade cooking range.

Continuing the intimacy of the dining room, the kitchen is tucked into a corner of the house, anchored by a large center island that serves as a work surface and seating area. The floor is made of reclaimed wooden planks, and copper accents play on the swirled colors in Montana travertine countertops. With its unusual furnishings—a blue Scandinavian hutch, a country table, a farmhouse lantern—the kitchen reflects a casual style and a life of collecting.

The owner's passion for antiques is evident in the home. Antique stained-glass windows are inset into a wall in the dining room and are used as transoms above the bedroom doors; vintage European fabrics have been incorporated into a delicate Victorian-inspired guestroom; handmade lace adorns mullioned windows; and kitschy swinging saloon doors open to a closet in the master suite. The owner's tasteful eye transfers to an eclectic style that pervades every nook of the 5,500-square-foot house.

On the second level, rough, weathered, reclaimed barn wood and timbers line the walls along the open walkway that overlooks the great room. This transitional space creates the feeling of strolling down an Old West boardwalk. Each of the floor's rooms has a different theme, from a child's log cabin bedroom, to guest quarters that resemble a Victorian hotel room, to the sophisticated elegance of the master bedroom.

The owner worked closely with a stonemason to achieve the central fireplace's rubble-rock effect, preferring the Harlowton stone to appear as though it had tumbled from a cliff rather than the more common symmetry. Other interesting design features incorporate the owner's eclectic style, including an upper-level walkway made of recycled barn wood that re-creates the feel of an Old West boardwalk.

The ceiling lowers in the dining room to create intimacy around a turned-leg farm table. Washed brick applied to a central wall and small fireplace hearth echoes the European heritage that the owner envisioned shaping the experience of a homesteading family who had immigrated to the region a century ago. Antique stained-glass windows were inset into the brick wall that divides the space from the front entry.

Using the muted tones of green willow and the pale hues of sunrise, the master bedroom is secretive and romantic. A high-canopy bed with flowing feminine fabric offsets the masculine language of the stone fireplace and the rough mantle reclaimed from a Montana mineshaft. Cool green distressed raised panels line the room's walls, and a set of double glass doors opens out to a shady balcony.

In the master bath, a brick floor again recalls European roots and has the effect of a garden path, leading to the ornate wrought-iron gate that was retrofitted as a shower door. An antique claw-foot tub and the cut-crystal pulls on the cabinetry add touches of elegance to the space.

The inspired treatment of antique, reclaimed architectural details gives this home an artfully

More brickwork surrounds the cooking hearth in the kitchen and ties the dining room's architectural element to this space. An apron-front sink hints at farmhouse beginnings, while a work island in the middle of the kitchen is clad in extremely modern stainless steel, hammered on the edges with handmade antique nails.

understated sophistication. That artistic touch extends outside, where French doors open to a generous porch. Hand-bent willow chairs and Amish rockers line the outdoor living space, which is flanked by shady covered areas. Seamlessly creating a flow between indoor and outdoor living, here the house becomes at once Adirondack and Western—woodsy and remote.

On the porch you can hear the creek and see the meadow that stretches to the woods that rise to the sky, which on a clear day holds that promised view of the mountains.

Weathered barn wood and a high transom made from a Victorian stained-glass window set the tone for the guest bedroom's decor. Washed in white, the room upholds the owner's love of vintage, which is reflected in the lace curtains, antique dress, and handmade quilt. Architecturally, the dark stained timbers in this room accentuate the planked walls and ceiling, mirroring elements of a traditional outbuilding in a new form.

Floral patterns and soft shades of green and cream set a romantic tone in the master suite. A wrought-iron bed is draped with a canopy of gauzy fabric to filter out the bright light of Montana mornings. The custom-made wainscot was hand-painted and antiqued to the owner's specifications.

Continuing the romantic atmosphere of the master suite, the bathroom has the aura of a garden retreat. A classic cast-iron tub sits atop the brick floor, which is set on a diagonal like a backyard path. The filigree of an arched botanical gate was retrofitted to create a whimsical design around the shower.

**CHAPTER 9**

# ROUGH
# AND REFINED

Photography by J K Lawrence

Perched high in the hills along the northwestern corner of Montana's Paradise Valley is a house that looks as though it has always been there.

Up there, the juniper and cypress trees gnarl into the rocky slopes. It seems an unlikely place for people to live, but the building hints at another purpose. Successive rooflines stepped into the hillside and a tower near the highest point allude to a nineteenth-century mining camp. In fact, this valley has authentic ties to gold mining in the 1860s and, later, lucrative coal

**Opposite: Heavy weathered wood, rusted metal, and makeshift shingles create a roughly textured exterior that contrasts with the sleek lines of the interior spaces.**

mining that brought the Northern Pacific Railroad into Montana Territory. Within this historical context, the house seems to be a natural fit in the rugged landscape.

"It was important to me to make this house look like something that belonged there," said the owner, who began his love affair with Montana when he came to fish the local spring creeks in 1982.

The mining camp concept came from Big Timberworks founder Merle Adams in the early design stage of the house. He collaborated with architect

Brian Brothers, AIA, as well as with the home owner to craft a uniquely intimate retreat.

"I had this idea that on the outside it would look like an old mine building that had been reclaimed, and inside it would feel like someone had retrofitted an industrial space into living space," Adams said. Brothers, who was an industrial designer prior to his architecture career, took the suggestion and applied it with the eye of a sculptor. The plan resonated with the owner immediately.

Standing on the threshold, heavy weathered wood posts, rusted metal board and batten, thick makeshift shingles, and a planked entry combine for the effect of an encampment cobbled together over time. There's a deserted aura to the place that comes from being up so high, but as the mahogany-stained, ladder-panel door opens, all this rough texture outside contradicts the refreshing sleek lines inside. Soft daylight floods the space and invites you into the house, where you are soothed by the smooth plaster walls and dark karri wood floor.

The owner's collection of art is displayed in thoughtful contrast to the contemporary leanings of the home: Works by Native American Montana painters Kevin Red Star and Rocky Hawkins punctuate the regional ties that came into play in the creation

Successive rooflines and a tower near the highest point allude to nineteenth-century industrial structures.

Big Timberworks crafted the cobbled look of this highland house in the spirit of early cabins that were constructed of found materials and meant to be temporary shelters.

of this eclectic living space. In the main room, a large acrylic painting by Red Star depicts an Indian warrior moving stealthily across the prairie, his face paint highlighting a sinister look in his eyes. Titled *Snake in the Grass*, the lifelike image adds action to the light-filled room.

The dry blond grass outside bends in a west wind and leans toward the valley floor, where a pasture holds the circular marks of a thresher that cut hay last fall. Beyond that field is Highway 89—the two-lane road

that leads south to Yellowstone National Park. Over it all loom the Yellowstone River and the mountains on the opposite side, a lineup of guardians beginning with Livingston Peak and continuing to Black Mountain, Mount Cowan, and Emigrant Peak. As you gaze quietly over this fantastic topography, it is easy to imagine the Indian of that painting, creeping through the grass in defense of this grand territory.

The main living space adjoins the kitchen, sitting, and dining area in an open floor plan. On the

The smooth curve of the wheat-colored plaster wall in the entry is an elegant contrast to some of the rough wood elements throughout the house.

Combined modernist elements of wood, metal, concrete, and stone add to the eclectic ambiance. Reusing old materials in different ways was a priority for the builder, architect, and home owner, not only for aesthetic value but also as a reflection of sustainable building practices.

far wall, a vignette of windows artistically frames the landscape. Crediting an Asian urban design "trick," Brothers staggered different-sized windows, trimmed with crisp white milk-paint, in a way that creates pastoral scenes that are as graphic as original oil paintings. One window holds the clear sheen of blue sky, edged in dark mountains, while another centers on a trio of navy blue grain silos to

the north. The effect is artful, but also grounded in the practical. Since the house is posed on a hillside, it is often buffeted by strong prevailing winds, and smaller windows are less likely to be damaged by the pressure of the extreme gusts so prevalent here.

"The basic interior premise was to be very urban, to give it a loft style," explained Brothers. "It's very different from the typical rustic cowboy style."

Due to its modest 2,700-square-foot size, the house has an intimate feel, just like a traditional cabin might have. Vaulted ceilings are buffered with exposed timbers, which are sculptural in detail yet comforting in their natural tone. The kitchen is open and welcoming, with its soft soapstone countertop and central cooking island. The living room is open to the kitchen, but a collection of relaxed chairs and a small gas stove makes it feel removed from the main flow of the house.

Although the owner and his wife worked with a local interior designer from Montana Expressions, there is a personal element to this home that can't be "designed." It comes from days spent antiquing and a taste for furnishings with a romantic flair, rather than a defined theme. In the master bedroom, for instance, the luxe burgundy coverings on the high bed contrast with a cowhide chair in the corner and clean-lined machinist bedside lights on the walls. Another example occurs in the guest suite, above the garage, where rice-paper Japanese shoji doors and an ornate divan are juxtaposed with a delicately hued Russell Chatham landscape painting.

"The house is a study of contrast—of rough and refined," observed Adams while walking through the home. He pointed out design elements with a sense of propriety: the curved burn marks on a header beam that was reclaimed from a warehouse fire; the cable handrail running downstairs that was once a chairlift line at Bridger Bowl; the elaborate pressed tin used on the kitchen island, taken from the ceiling of a dilapidated farmhouse on the Montana–North Dakota border. Each piece of this home has a story and Adams knows them all, noting that every material in the house is on its second or third life.

Applying an Asian urban design "trick," architect Brian Brothers framed different views of the surrounding landscape with windows of varying sizes in the dining room.

This premise—the salvage and resurrection of building materials into new forms—is the foundation of Adams's Big Timberworks. Back in 1983, when Adams co-founded the company, the focus was on building log-and-timber homes. Through the

years the business grew and then morphed to focus on customized creations, in addition to timber-frame structures. Using recycled and reclaimed materials, the craftsmen at Big Timberworks mill siding, posts, and beams; construct frames and trusses; and hand-craft one-of-a-kind furniture and lighting, among other tasks. The design-build projects are where the Big Timberworks team has the opportunity to show-case all of its talent and embrace the creative process from conceptualization to completion.

Throughout the mining camp–inspired house there are degrees of edginess that challenge the clas-sic aesthetic of architectural design in Montana: The reused materials tie in with contemporary environ-mental values; the historic vernacular context of the mining structure borrows from another era; and the combined modernist elements of wood, metal, con-crete, and stone add to the eclectic ambiance. This is far from cowboy chic. In fact, Big Timberworks has hit on a style all its own—call it an emerging style that falls somewhere within the monikers "mod-ern rustic" or "rustic industrial." No matter how it's labeled, it fits this place and embodies an uncommon collective creativity.

In the end, Adams, who loves junkyard trea-sures and the texture of all things wood; Brothers, who relishes clean, industrial lines; and the owner, who enjoys a kind of analytical luxury, melded their ideas of a perfect retreat with talent, intuitive design, and trust.

The incorporation of industrial materials—corrugated metal and concrete floors—into a downstairs bathroom conveys a modern approach.

Opposite: The open, welcoming kitchen features a soft soapstone countertop and central cooking island. Antique pressed tin, reclaimed from an old farmhouse, accents the island and the kitchen backsplash.

Leaning toward stately with its high canopy bed and burgundy velvet bed coverings, the master bedroom is a contrast to some of the rustic elements found elsewhere in the house.

Opposite: The guest room on the second level is a departure from the home's Euro-eclectic decor. Here, rice-paper shoji doors and a settee add an Asian touch. Exposed ductwork gives the space the feel of an urban loft.

## CHAPTER 10

# MODERN HOMESTEAD

Photography by Gordon Gregory

It you take the time to look closely at Montana's landscape, the expanse of it becomes meditative: the open spaces of lowland valleys, rhythmic with hayfields and fence lines; the gently sloping foothills; the mountains rising into the sky. David and Julie Finegan didn't want to forget that soothing sensation and connection to place when they built their home in the Gallatin Valley.

"You want the sense of a roof over your head that makes you feel protected from the elements, but you don't want to feel disconnected," said David.

When the couple approached architect Stephen Dynia of Dynia Architects in Jackson, Wyoming, they told him they wanted a home with a long line to capture surrounding mountain views, and they wanted to keep it small and simple. Simplicity, for the Finegans, manifested in a fresh, contemporary style.

Having lived in a historic 1908 Neoclassical four-square home in Denver, they did not want a house that was fussy. Inspired by the form and shape

Opposite: In the spirit of traditional cabins, this house was intended to appear as if the original house had been added on to over time using new materials and dimensions. The rafters of the roof draw attention by using symmetry as a functional and ornamental element.

The agricultural leanings of the home are brought into focus with an old-fashioned hay thresher in the foreground.

of agricultural structures in this valley—the barns, sheep sheds, and cabins—the Finegans blended elements from each to create their vision of the modern homestead.

To soften the modern parallel and perpendicular lines of the house, Dynia called upon vernacular elements that appear in utilitarian buildings throughout the region. Clad in tobacco-colored board and batten, there's the gabled farmhouse shape of the two-level section that is anchored by the bedroom, bath, and home office spaces. On the main level, the low profile of a shed-style structure mirrors the loafing sheds in the region. Pale stonework speaks of the light-colored limestone cliffs on the valley's fringe. And corrugated metal on the roof reflects the practical nature of agricultural buildings.

On the outside, the home's texture reflects its natural surroundings. Stepping inside, there is very little separation from the immediate landscape. The main living space is spanned by a long line of southern-exposure windows that work to seamlessly connect the house with the tall grass outside and to the distant mountains.

Unlike traditional cabins that were often small and dark, this home in the country opens to the warmth of the southern exposure that fills the main living space from sunup until sundown. The materials—wood, stone, and glass—are true to the natural elements that have been used in construction for centuries, though they are applied here in a much more contemporary way.

Running east to west, architect Stephen Dynia opened the house to light and the outdoor environment from point to point.

"We wanted the inside to flow outward," said Julie, "so we chose a darker floor and kept it consistent throughout the house to keep the spaces uniform and streamlined."

At only 2,900 square feet, the flowing design makes the house feel expansive, but the space is as pragmatic as any small cabin. The couple chose all natural materials: walnut floors, alder trim around windows and doors, rough glue-lam beams, stone. They tried to use healthy materials for the interior, such as low-VOC paints to minimize off-gassing,

and natural fibers in furnishings and rugs.

The galley-style kitchen is masterfully efficient without feeling confined. Custom bamboo cabinets by Crown Creations of Livingston reinforce the sustainable intentions of the owners, and a trio of amber-colored, hand-blown glass canister lights hang over the kitchen island for ambient lighting.

Around the corner, a straight-lined dining room table beckons guests and reinforces the casual style of the home. Just a few steps away are two fawn-colored sofas that center on the stone fireplace. The rooms

Delicate hand-blown glass canister lights hang over the central island in the galley-style kitchen.

A painting by Montana artist Russell Chatham sets the living room's color scheme of crisp but earthy blue and golden yellow.

A stone dividing wall in the dining area brings out the organic aspect of the interior spaces.

maximize space by employing overlapping functions —the living and dining areas and kitchen are connected, eliminating transition spaces such as hallways and dividing walls. The furnishings, from Eco-Terric in Bozeman, are spare yet comfortable. Warm yellow- and blue-accented pillows and a bright rug add a jolt of color to the room, as does a large Russell Chatham lithograph.

But always, there is the light, moving from the kitchen window on the eastern end of the room to the far western window in the master bedroom. The time of day dictates the atmosphere in the room, from the warm light of the morning, to the heat of midday, to the coolness of the night that draws the couple out onto the deck to enjoy the stars near the warmth of the outdoor fireplace. The result is a home with an honesty that emulates Big Sky Country.

"What makes the concept of the house work is the way our lifestyle relates to the land," David said. "There's little division between inside and outside."

Just off the kitchen, a covered deck extends the living space outside and takes the owners back into the natural landscape.

A complete departure from the traditional cabin, this modern version maintains the spirit of seclusion while allowing daylight to flood every room in the house.

CHAPTER 11

# MONTANA
# MICRO CABINS

Photography by Lynn Donaldson

As Charles Finn picks his way through the Heritage Timber salvage yard in Potomac, he sees more than scraps of wood. For him, a single element—a heavy beam, an antique door, a picture window—can inspire the entire form of one of his micro cabins. A window with vintage wavy glass becomes the launching point for a writing studio; a heap of discarded tractor gears becomes doorknobs; a stack of weathered, twisted lumber becomes floorboards in one of his one-room custom cabins.

One part necessity, one part whimsy, and all parts artistic, Finn has created a string of quirky retreats in the last few years that echo his experience living in a seven-by-twelve-foot handmade cabin in Argenta, British Columbia. He also draws on his travels to Japan and India, where, respectively, smaller homes are the norm and reusing everything is a necessity. He is a writer by craft, but by trade he has become a thoughtful designer and careful builder of Montana micro cabins.

Utilizing handpicked reclaimed and recycled materials, each cabin is an original creation that ranges in size from seven by twelve feet to nine by fourteen feet. That's partly because working with salvaged materials makes dimensions unpredictable or, in some cases, serendipitous. Finn works with Gary Delp at Heritage Timber, taking down old buildings around Montana. What Heritage discards—because it is too old, too twisted, too discolored, or simply not

available in a large enough quantity—Finn crafts into one-of-a-kind retreats.

Rarely using a board longer than eight feet, Finn wrestles with the fine line of creating a living space that is cozy but not claustrophobic. The cabins work well for people who are looking for a unique guesthouse, home office, art studio, or off-the-grid retreat.

"I'm a big proponent of living little," claims Finn. "I think there's a bit of hermit in all of us, and everyone wants to go back to the woods."

The scent of wood and sawdust from freshly planed boards permeates his shop. He just walked the lumberyard for inspiration and found a stack of wood that will construct the floor of his next project. On the concrete he has laid out the jigsaw puzzle framework of that cabin. "This one is going to be a little bigger," he says. It will have a small sleeping loft, maybe a porch, and it might provide twelve by fourteen feet of living space. Maybe.

Inspired by the experience of living in a custom-built caravan, artisan Charles Finn decided to experiment with his own micro cabin, a compact capsule of respite. It now serves as his writing studio, where all the necessities of creativity are within an arm's reach.

The earliest cabins were small, simple, and pragmatic. Although each of these getaways reflects a minimalist approach that reads as a very modern aesthetic, the fact that they are constructed of salvaged materials selected specifically for small spaces actually defines them as authentic cabins.

# CABIN IN THE WOODS

Finn's own cabin is a rustic and functional abode tucked into a quiet patch of ponderosa pines. Crude wooden steps lead up to the door, which has a handle made from an old tractor gear. The oval door is an ode to the diminutive dwellings described in *The Hobbit*. Inside, wide well-worn plank floors slip beneath the built-in bed, writing table, and wood-burning stove. Most everything is within easy reach, with essentials stowed in various built-in cabinets or under the bed in storage containers, as efficiently as a ship's cabin.

The ceiling truss was once the crossbar of a telephone pole, and the holes where the glass transformers rested are still visible. The only adornments are red-painted window trim and a wide ledge that runs along the wall as a catwalk for Finn's companion kitty to see outside. The aged wood, each piece with its own history, warmly wraps around the room, drawing the soft sunlight inside. Otherwise, the fully insulated room is spare, yet intimate. The space initially requires careful movement and a series of calculated efforts not to step on toes or to bump the corners of the bed, counter, or table. But after a while, it simply feels comfortable.

"People see it and think that it's small—too small," admits Finn. "But once you live in it you realize that you can make do with so much less."

There is no running water. Finn cooks on an old Coleman gas stove, reads by lamplight, and powers his computer with an inverter that has deep-sea cell batteries. The outhouse is a short walk in the woods. Finn lived here for two years, though now he uses it mainly as a writing studio. He calls the simplicity "a soulful way of living."

Situated in the middle of a Flathead Valley field framed by the Mission Range, the gypsy caravan serves as an escape for the owners. Utilizing reclaimed farmhouse clapboard siding, a tin roof, and small windows, the tiny abode reflects the authentic resourcefulness manifested in the early cabins that once dotted this farmland.

# KISMET CABIN

For Lori Parr Campbell, the sage green and cranberry red cabin she saw at the Missoula Farmers' Market was the answer to her many questions about building a temporary house on her Flathead Valley property. She was charmed by the scale of the seven-by-twelve-foot carpenter's gem that Charles Finn had hauled on a trailer to sell at the weekly market. A petite woman, it seemed to suit her perfectly, and she almost bought it on the spot.

After a week of deliberation, she bought the cabin along with a smaller version that she uses as an art studio. Now she says it was "kismet," meant to be hers all along.

Resembling a gypsy caravan, the cabin sits in a swale on Campbell's parcel of land, dubbed Rosalie Ranch in honor of her mother. She and her husband use it often as a retreat from the growing urbanism of Missoula, where they live in a historic two-bedroom

Inside the cabin is an intimate glimpse into the owners' hideout. Lavender bundles, books, whimsical pictures, and found objects pepper the interior that is lit only by lamplight. The built-in bed frames a standard double mattress, and light filtered through skylights and windows keep the small space from seeming claustrophobic.

railroad bungalow. The cabin seems to be the only structure in a vast landscape, with the Mission Range mountains towering in the distance and a sea of farmland unfurling in every direction.

The interim getaway has allowed the couple the luxury of time as they plan to build a larger main house. They've walked the acreage; observed the cycle of seasons and the plants that grow here; learned of the coyotes, elk, songbirds, and the badger den—they've learned the lay of the land.

Open the red oval-shaped door, and the scent of smudged lavender wafts into the air. An organic farmer, Campbell's main crop is lavender—ribbon-tied bunches and bundles of flowers dry inside the cabin. The tiny room is a display case of personal sundries: a farmer's scythe, images of fairies, a St. Francis of Assisi icon, a delicately spun bird's nest still attached to a willow branch perched above in the skylight. Books are stacked on the built-in half-moon table and on the shelves that frame the bed.

Finn's workmanship and care is apparent, in each wooden-pegged nail hole and in the neatly lined wall of short-dimension fir. Lined with various species of wood from floor to ceiling, the cabin is a capsule of privacy and quietude. From here the couple watches meteor showers and listens to snow settling on the metal roof. A tiny gas stove keeps the space warm at any time of the year.

Sided with clapboards that were once on a farmhouse in New York, the structure has an old-fashioned allure. It beckons people to huddle around it, to enjoy the view, to listen to the soft sounds of the valley. Campbell often pauses to notice the details that show in Finn's craftsmanship.

"It feels like a boat," she reflects. "I feel like I'm in a little ship sailing across the prairie."

No two are alike: The shingled cabins near Moiese sit in the shade of hundred-year-old cottonwoods. The owners kept the structures small and simple out of respect for the open space surrounding the property.

# HAYFIELD HIDEOUT

Dotting the Montana landscape are buildings that influence Charles Finn's micro cabins: a board and batten woodshed, a dilapidated barn, a weathered farmhouse. There are agricultural buildings with rolled roofs, abandoned homestead cabins, and pole barns cobbled together with materials that were once readily available and cheap. Finn embraces his projects with more artistry, perhaps, but his practical premise is the same.

Similarly, Rafael Chacone and Andy Laue were also swayed by the farm structures and simple homes around their property near the National Bison Range in Moiese. When they commissioned Finn to build two cabins on their hayfield acreage, they wanted the structures to have a light footprint on the land.

"We wanted these cabins to look like they'd always been part of the landscape, not an eyesore of

Built for functionality entirely from salvaged materials, the two cabins provide the owners with separate living spaces. At nine by fourteen feet each, the buildings provide all the room the owners need in a rural retreat from bustling urban lives.

A thick piece of wood from a cottonwood tree becomes a desk.

Inside the dining cabin, a set of shelves holds vintage Fiestaware and Bauer bowls—designer icons of outdoor living from the 1950s. A clerestory window runs the length of the cabin to allow soft light to warm the room.

new materials or elements that don't belong here," Chacone explained.

Chacone is an art historian specializing in American architecture, specifically rural structures, which he reveres as the architecture of the common man and woman. As a result, he and Laue drew up plans for the structures and worked with Finn to find materials from Missoula's Home Resource, a recycled building material center.

The elements they purchased defined the shape of each cabin. For comfort, the couple wanted to divide the functions of living, so one structure is the kitchen cabin and the other is the sleeping cabin. Both buildings' dimensions are nine by four feet, and both feature the luxury of electricity. Chacone jokes that they look like some combination of an espresso cart and an old sheepherder's wagon.

Siting the cabins was crucial to the creation of the welcoming feeling here. Finn and his clients intentionally placed them in the shade of the hundred-year-old cottonwood shelterbelt. The covered porch is the focus upon arriving at the cabins. Chacone and Laue built this addition for sentimental reasons, re-creating Laue's childhood memory of standing on his grandmother's porch that faced west toward a stand of cottonwoods on her property in Nebraska.

A reclaimed cabinet set the width of the kitchen cabin, its shelves now stacked with Fiestaware, pots and pans, vintage ceramic Bauer bowls, and mason jars that are used as drinking glasses. A window over the sink looks out onto an alfalfa field and the rolling hills of the Bison Range, and a raised clerestory runs the length of the cabin's ceiling, allowing light to shine over the exposed timbers. In the corner, the top of the gas stove is decorated with found stones—heart-shaped, variegated, smooth.

Across the deck to the sleeping cabin, a picture window brings the outdoors into the cozy space that is heated by a small propane stove. The owners spend time here reading, journaling, and just basically relaxing.

Cedar planks span the floor, and the walls are constructed of wood that was once part of a goat shed near Potomac.

The sleeping cabin space was defined by another reclaimed element: the large picture window that now looks toward the Mission Range. A thick, planed piece of wood from a cottonwood tree is mounted to the wall for use as a desk. The bed is framed by two antique posts that came from a historic Craftsman home. There is a peaceful feeling in the space, with the worn wood materials creating an atmosphere that is warm and comforting.

The two cabins are connected by a deck that forms a shelter and frames the landscape. Chacone and Laue spend leisurely time here at an antique table drinking morning coffee as the sun comes up, or dining under the stars with friends at night. Out here, time is marked by the cycle of daylight, by basic needs. Chacone likens it to the pleasures of a month-long hiking trip that he and Laue took in the mountains of Spain, when the primary task of the day was to put on boots and start walking. That simplicity is prevalent at their cabins, too.

"It's more about spending time outside when we are here," says Chacone. "The idea is to see this place as a retreat and to minimize contact with the outside world. It's another step in the direction of simplifying our lives."

The openness of the surrounding farmland as seen from the deck between the cabins inspires many quiet afternoons of reading and lively dinner parties under the stars.

# RESOURCES

## CHAPTER 1
### RETRO COZY

*Photography*
Gordon Gregory Photography
94 West Fieldview Circle
Bozeman, MT 59715
(406) 556-9854
www.gordongregoryphoto.com

*Contractor*
Swanson Construction
P.O. Box 6538
Bozeman, MT 59771
(406) 587-8200
www.swansonconstruction.net

*Interior Design*
Carol Smith, owner
ccsmt9999@aol.com

## CHAPTER 2
### DOUBLE D RANCH

*Photography*
Gordon Gregory Photography
94 West Fieldview Circle
Bozeman, MT 59715
(406) 556-9854
www.gordongregoryphoto.com

*Architecture*
Miller Architects PC
Candace Tillotson-Miller, principal
208 West Park Street
Livingston, MT 59047
(406) 222-7057
www.ctmarchitects.com

*Contractor*
Yellowstone Traditions
Harry Howard, principal
Justin Bolind, project manager
34290 East Frontage Road
Bozeman, MT 59715
(406) 587-0968
www.yellowstonetraditions.com

*Interior Design*
Diana Beattie Interiors
1136 Fifth Avenue
New York, NY 10128
(212) 722-6226

## CHAPTER 3
### CANYON RESPITE

*Photography*
Roger Wade Studio
19583 Highway 83
Bigfork, MT 59911
(800) 507-6437
www.rogerwadestudio.com

*Architecture*
Locati Architects
Jerry Locati, principal
Kyle Tage, project manager and partner
1007 East Main Street, Suite 202
Bozeman, MT 59715
(406) 587-1139
www.locatiarchitects.com

*Contractor*
Schlauch Bottcher Construction
2010 Gilkerson Drive
Bozeman, MT 59715
(406) 585-0735
www.sbconstruction.com

*Interior Design*
Donna Brooks
Brooks Interior Design
670 Orlando Boulevard, Suite 1001
Maiteland, FL 32751
(407) 539-2655
www.brooksinteriordesign.com

## CHAPTER 4
## CELEBRATING THE BARN

*Photography*
Tom Ferris
219 East Story Avenue
Bozeman, MT 59715
(406) 587-3111
www.tomferris.com

*Architecture*
zimtor architecture
Thor Arnold and Gary Zimmer, principals
415 East Birch Street
Bozeman, MT 59715
(406) 582-1499
www.zimtor.com

*Contractor*
Clay Bowden Construction
712 West Clark Street
Livingston, MT 59047
(406) 222-8213

*Interior Design*
Montana Expressions
2504 West Main Street
Bozeman, MT 59715
(406) 585-5839
www.montanaexpressions.com

*Kitchen*
McPhie Cabinetry
435 East Main Street
Bozeman, MT 59715
(406) 586-1708
www.mcphiecabinetry.com

*Tulikivi Soapstone*
WarmStone Fireplaces and Designs
116 North B Street
Livingston, MT 59047
(406) 333-4383
www.warmstone.com

*Building Materials*
Durisol Building Systems, Inc.
67 Frid Street
Hamilton, Ontario
Canada L8P 4M3
(905) 521-0999
www.durisolbuild.com

## CHAPTER 5
## SPRINGHILL HIDEOUT

*Photography*
Roger Wade Studio
19583 Highway 83
Bigfork, MT 59911
(800) 507-6437
www.rogerwadestudio.com

*Architecture and Interior Design*
Locati Architects
Jerry Locati, principal
Kyle Tage, project manager and partner
1007 East Main Street, Suite 202
Bozeman, MT 59715
(406) 587-1139
www.locatiarchitects.com

*Contractor*
Schlauch Bottcher Construction
2010 Gilkerson Drive
Bozeman, MT 59715
(406) 585-0735
www.sbconstruction.com

**CHAPTER 6**
BIG SKY CABIN

*Photography*
Gordon Gregory Photography
94 West Fieldview Circle
Bozeman, MT 59715
(406) 556-9854
www.gordongregoryphoto.com

*Architecture*
Faure Halvorsen Architects
1425 West Main Street, Suite A
Bozeman, MT 59715
(406) 587-1204
www.faurehalvorsen.com

*Contractor*
Pat Johnson Construction Management Group
6935 Mogollon Drive
Bozeman, MT 59715
(406) 587-1649

*Interior Design*
Carole Sisson Designs
117 East Main Street
Bozeman, MT 59715
(406) 587-2600

Carole Sisson Designs–Big Sky
99 Lone Peak Drive
Big Sky Town Center
Big Sky, MT 59716
(406) 993-2666
www.sissondesigns.com

**CHAPTER 7**
COW CAMP STYLE

*Photography*
Gordon Gregory Photography
94 West Fieldview Circle
Bozeman, MT 59715
(406) 556-9854
www.gordongregoryphoto.com

*Architecture*
Miller Architects PC
Candace Tillotson-Miller, principal
Travis Denman, project manager
208 West Park Street
Livingston, MT 59047
(406) 222-7057
www.ctmarchitects.com

*Contractor*
Yellowstone Traditions
Harry Howard, principal
34290 East Frontage Road
Bozeman, MT 59715
(406) 587-0968
www.yellowstonetraditions.com

*Interior Design*
Diana Beattie Interiors
1136 Fifth Avenue
New York, NY 10128
(212) 722-6226

**CHAPTER 8**
VINTAGE CHARM

*Photography*
Roger Wade Studio
19583 Highway 83
Bigfork, MT 59911
(800) 507-6437
www.rogerwadestudio.com

*Architecture*
Joseph Magaddino Architecture
P.O. Box 1151
Bigfork, MT 59911
(406) 837-1220
www.magaddinoarchitecture.com

*Contractor*
Denman Construction
Craig Denman, president
3927 Highway 40 West
Box 5420
Whitefish, MT 59937
(406) 863-9925
www.denmanconstruction.com

**CHAPTER 9**
ROUGH AND REFINED

*Photography*
J K Lawrence Photography, Inc.
Architectural and Interiors Photography
96 Vita Court
Bozeman, MT 59718
(406) 686-4189
www.jklawrencephoto.com

*Architecture*
Brian H. Brothers
One Rabel Lane
Gallatin Gateway, MT 59730
(406) 539-6275
http://web.mac.com/brianbrothers

*Contractor*
Big Timberworks
One Rabel Lane
Gallatin Gateway, MT 59730
(406) 763-4639 or (800) 763-4639
www.bigtimberworks.com

*Interior Design*
Montana Expressions
2504 West Main Street
Bozeman, MT 59715
(406) 585-5839
www.montanaexpressions.com

## CHAPTER 10
## MODERN HOMESTEAD

*Photography*
Gordon Gregory Photography
94 West Fieldview Circle
Bozeman, MT 59715
(406) 556-9854
www.gordongregoryphoto.com

*Architecture*
Dynia Architects
Stephen Dynia, principal
1135 Maple Way
Jackson, WY 83001
(307) 733-3766
www.dynia.com

*Contractor*
Bridger Builders
Jim and Lois Syth
115 West Kagy Boulevard
Bozeman, MT 59715
(406) 587-8544

*Interior Design*
Eco-Terric
716 East Mendenhall Street
Bozeman, MT 59715
(406) 586-7643
www.eco-terric.com

*Landscape Design*
Valley of the Flowers
609 Quaws Boulevard
Belgrade, MT 59714
(406) 388-1290
www.valleyoftheflowers.com

*Cabinetry*
Crown Creations Cabinetmakers
110 North N Street
Livingston, MT 59047
(406) 222-7262

## CHAPTER 11
## MONTANA MICRO CABINS

*Photography*
Lynn Donaldson
215 East Lewis Street, Studio 104
Livingston, MT 59047
(406) 570-9146
www.lynndonaldson.com

*Builder*
A Room of One's Own
Charles Finn
Stevensville, MT
(406) 239-1519